Behind Every Dark Cloud

A Caregiver's Heart

BERNITA A. GLENN

authorHOUSE®

AuthorHouse™
1663 Liberty Drive
Bloomington, IN 47403
www.authorhouse.com
Phone: 1-800-839-8640

Published by AuthorHouse   04/09/2013

ISBN: 978-1-4817-3518-6 (sc)
ISBN: 978-1-4817-3517-9 (e)

Library of Congress Control Number: 2013905808

All Scripture quotations in this book are taken from the Holy Bible, King James
Version, Oral Roberts Edition, Copyright© 1981 by Oral Roberts Evangelistic
Association, Inc., Tulsa, Oklahoma unless otherwise stated.

This book is dedicated to my parents Deacon Julius and Mrs. Thelma Glenn, who consistently reminded me that it is so much better to give than to receive.

Contents

Preface xi

Introduction - Caregiving 101 xv

1. Finding Yourself in the Midst of Chaos 1

2. Why Me? 10

3. Nothing Eases Pain like a Good Cry 14

4. The Struggle for Perfection 18

5. If You Don't Take Care of You, Who Will? 22

6. A Mother's Love 26

7. Living with Dad 30

8. In Our Darkest Hour God Will Send an Angel 36

9. Give Love, Always 39

10. Forgiveness 43

11. There Is a Joy in Giving 46

12. Relax—Make Yourself a Priority 49

13. You're entitled to A Stress Free Life 52

14. When Your Faith Is Tested 55

15. "Scriptures to Savor" 58

Acknowledgements

*In all your ways acknowledge Him, and He
shall direct your paths. Proverbs 3:6 NKJV*

I thank God for the honor and privilege of providing care for both my mother and father and for revealing to me the many joys associated with serving others.

With special thanks:

❖ To my Pastor, Rev. Dr. Alvin Love, thanks so much for posing the crucial question, "If you don't take care of you, who will?" Those nine little words were significant to my survival as a Caregiver and I will be sure to share them as I converse with others on the same journey.

❖ To my valuable friends Mrs. Pamela Buchanan-Long, Mrs. Bessie Hampton, Mother Lottie Yates, for contributing time to review my manuscript and offering editing ideas. I am so grateful for your encouraging words.

❖ To my precious childhood friend and publisher, Mrs. Judith GrandPre'-Smith who extended her expertise in editing, evaluating and encouraging me on this, my first manuscript. I could have never done it without you.

❖ To Mrs. Jennifer Gaidos, a great English instructor and proofreader. Your willingness to read every word, dot every "i", cross every "t" and insert every comma and period is very much appreciated. Thank you so much for stepping in to quickly assist me in this project.

❖ To my wonderful and supportive children, Albert Jerome and Leslie Renee, who continually inspire me to reach for the stars and realize my dream to become a published author. You are the jewels that shine brightly in my heart.

This book is written for the purpose of encouraging Caregivers throughout the world—those who readily put their lives on hold to care, comfort and console a loved one in a time of need.

I encourage you to pray for one another. No one can truly understand the challenges you face except a brother or sister Caregiver who has walked in your shoes. Be blessed in knowing that through it all, certainly, *Behind Every Dark Cloud* is a silver lining.

God strengthen you on your journey!

Preface

P rayer is a gift you give to yourself and others. When you pray, you commune with God and connect so that you can tap into your indwelling strength. This process enables you to forge ahead with confidence and conviction as you navigate through any change or challenge.

When a person dear to you is in need, you can help them through prayer, patience and perseverance. The power of faith and understanding are also useful tools to free your mind, heart and spirit of fear, frustration and fatigue.

Life can be full of endless tasks, tensions and transitions along with an infinite number of places to go and things to do. In the midst of everything, take time to savor the wonders of life and living. As you move through each day, remember to build a strong circle of friends and family for support, encouragement and love.

We are all spiritual beings growing in awareness through personal and painful experiences. At the close of each day, give thanks for being able to serve and being blessed in return.

> *I expect to pass through this world but once. Any good thing therefore that I can do or any kindness that I can show to any fellow creature, let me do it now; let me not defer it or neglect it, for I shall not pass this way again.*
>
> *-Etienne De Grellet*
>
> *(French Quaker Missionary)*

"*Joy*"

By Ashley Cleveland | from the album
God Don't Never Change

Behind every dark cloud There's a silver lining
After each rainstorm There's a bright new start
When troubles grieve you And friends deceive you
Oh don't worry it'll pass over
In the morning

When trials pull your heartstrings Don't be discouraged
And even though pain and misery Fill your eyes with tears
These trials will soon pass And soon they will depart
O alleluia they will pass over
By and by

And remember

Weeping may endure for a night
But joy, joy, joy, joy
Joy, joy will come
Joy, joy joy, joy joy, joy joy

Introduction

Caregiving 101
(A world made just for you)

This is how we know what love is: Jesus
Christ laid down his life for us. And we
ought to lay down our lives for our brothers.
If anyone has material possessions and
sees his brother in need but has no pity on
him, how can the love of God be in him?
Let us not love with words or tongue but
with actions and in truth. 1 John 3:16-18

Congratulations on taking some time away from your busy schedule to spend what I call "quality time with self." Time is a comforting instrument of life but as Caregivers there never seems to be enough of that to go around. There is seldom time for rest because in most cases our minds are in a constant thought pattern. When the opportunity comes for those quiet moments to finally present themselves, we are often filled with thoughts of *I need to be doing this* or *I need to be doing that*. Free time is enjoyed in quick segments. With that in mind, let me once again welcome you into this short respite. I would like to share some lessons on caregiving and allow you to recognize some *"aha"* moments that will encourage you along your journey.

Whether you spend the majority of your day caring for a sick child, a parent with Alzheimer's, a sibling with a debilitating disease or a loved one battling cancer, you will come to realize that between the stresses of the day, there must also be time for yourself. I can only imagine that your reason for being in this special moment is because you are in search of something. Perhaps you are searching for a refuge, a sense of understanding, a shoulder to cry on or some small miracle to reward you in your life as a Caregiver. This book is certainly no magical cure for your specific situation; however, it is full of encouragement, biblical passages and a few funny tales to hopefully brighten your day. Finding that you are not alone on this journey and realizing that others have experiences similar to yours will open a whole new way of thinking and perhaps even prompt you into sharing your story to help others. You may find that sharing is the best method for releasing the stresses that come from giving care. The materials within these pages are meant to help minimize the heartbreaks and headaches that you face as a Caregiver.

So come on! Jump in, and join me on a journey through the pages of what I call *Caregivers 101* as I share my experiences and encourage you with ways to make life easier and much more enjoyable.

Be blessed.

Chapter One

Finding Yourself in the Midst of Chaos
(Who Am I, Really?)

Nay, in all these things we are
more than conquerors through Him
that loved us. Romans 8:37

As Caregivers we often lose ourselves in the hustle and bustle of the everyday tasks of giving. My first experience as a Caregiver came when my mother was diagnosed with bone cancer in November of 1999. The doctor gave her six months to live, and I remember thinking just how callous this physician was to render such bad news during the festive holiday season. The look on my mother's face took on such a sadness, and I was so devastated with the news that I immediately put the brakes on my life and dedicated myself to taking care of her. I didn't realize the gravity of the task associated with rendering care, nor was I aware of the pitfalls that surrounded the role. As I fell into this role (and yes we do fall into it) and began to busily perform the many duties of giving care, winter faded, and the days began to show signs of spring before I realized the

1

magnitude of my situation; my life had been turned upside down in a matter of months.

What happened to my lease on life?

Taking care of my mother took up the majority of my time but she was an angel of a patient. Caring for her took so much time that I thought it best that I give up my apartment and move back home. This would cut down on travel time, both morning and evening, and make me more accessible to my mother. *NOT! What in God's name was I thinking?* Shortly after that move I realized that I had made a big mistake. (Mental note: Never give up your personal living quarters because that is your lifeline to sanity). Moving back home became a signal to others that I could handle everything and their help was no longer required. Soon after the move, caring for my mother was no longer a shared responsibility with my siblings. It became my personal duty. My presence in the home everyday gave others no reason to be there. Sound familiar? Someone reading these words can relate to what I am saying because you may have experienced the same scenario. Let me reiterate, *NEVER* give up your living quarters! Once you do that, you will have given up your safe haven. Momma once told me, "There is nothing in this world greater than peace of mind." Relinquish your privacy, and you will no longer have that quiet space to run to when there is the need to be alone. There will never be that "me time" to sit still, linger in the bath, take that much needed nap or read a book undisturbed. Never again will you have your private sanctuary to relax, put your feet up, let the telephone and door go unanswered or, if you desire, run naked through the hallways. Everyone will expect you to carry the torch for the duration of the race, and believe me, it can be a long and lonely journey to the finish line.

Feelings of abandonment

Let's face it, no one came to you and asked you to take on the responsibility of giving care, nor was it anyone's intention that you handle this task alone. It was your unconscious willingness coupled with compassion and a kind heart that led you to take on this role. People truly want to lend a helping hand but once you took the reins by making decisions, resolving issues, becoming the "in charge" person, the job became yours and yours alone. Your willingness to step in and provide such exceptional care has outweighed the choices of others and has given them the justification needed to bow out of the way, gracefully. They don't leave you to manage on your own out of spite. Most stand back because they feel inadequate and can't measure up to your standard of rendering care. Once people perceive that you are in control of things, *shift* happens. The visits and help become less frequent. People begin to pick up the pieces of their own lives and move on to other things, leaving you with a feeling of abandonment. Welcome to the world of caregiving!

I spent numerous hours searching for a reason as to why people take on or accept this role and I have come to the conclusion that caregiving is not something that we choose. However, it is something that we have been chosen to do. It is a role for which we have been chosen without prior knowledge or warning, a role that we were being prepared for over time. Perhaps one day you woke up and found yourself asking the question, "How did I get here?" Well, you're not alone in your query. There are thousands of us in the world who ask the same question. Caregiving is not an easy role to perform. In fact, most of us see it as one of the most thankless and unrewarding jobs in the world—one that can leave you wounded, tearful and broken. But, it can also be a joyful blessing if you stop to recognize your purpose. (We will talk more about joy in another chapter). Failure to understand your role as a Caregiver can fill you with such anxiety that you will become a stranger in your own body.

Coming face to face with the stranger

I was introduced to *the* stranger early one morning as I was routinely washing my face in the bathroom. As I paused to look in the mirror, I asked myself, "Who are you?" Over the past few months, the anxiety of giving care had transformed me into a monster. Prior to becoming a Caregiver, I took pleasure in my appearance. However, due to lack of time, that pleasure shifted, and I thought so little about my looks that I did not recognize the gradual change from beauty to beast, however, it was there in that mirror that I stared at the sadness. My eyes had become droopy, my hair was graying around the edges, wrinkles had replaced the smoothness around my mouth and mentally I had become a bitter and unhappy woman. I had allowed caregiving to take its toll on me and it had taken me to an unfamiliar place. I had become trapped in a body possessed by bitterness that transmuted into something unrecognizable. I took another look into the eyes which stared back at me in that mirror and asked again, "Who are you?" At that moment I believed that I was looking into the face of the devil himself. As that evil stranger starred back at me, I knew then that I had to stop the madness and do something to regain control over my life; the devil was indeed a liar.

That day was my official day to change and do something to save myself from self-destruction. I fell to my knees on the cold, tiled bathroom floor and cried until sanity returned, "God give me strength to overcome this battle," I prayed.

Those few moments of lying alone, in search of understanding, seemed like an eternity. No one saw me, no one heard me, and I believe that in that moment of metamorphosis, no one cared. I lay curled up, realizing that I was fighting a self-destructing battle—yet determined to win back my soul.

Recognizing others just like me

After picking myself up from the cold and icy floor, I received what I believe to be a revelation from the Holy Spirit Himself. I had come to the realization that I was not the *only* Caregiver in the world—there were others fighting the same dreadful battle. I recognized in that moment I had to share my story so that others would know they were not alone; there were others on this same Caregiver expedition. Praise the Lord, we're not alone! Let today be your official "day of change" to save yourself.

Stop complaining—think of the man with no feet

A friend of mine shared a story with me not too long ago. He was a mild-mannered person who portrayed an easy, no hustle and bustle type of life. He was always wearing a smile and would often provide a joke or two to make others laugh. One could not have imagined the worries that he was faced with on a daily basis. As part of a working crew, we developed a close relationship. Every day as we left the yard heading to our first job, he would redirect the driver to a different location. We would pull up to the re-directed address and he would get out of the truck and spend 15-20 minutes inside. This continued for several weeks before I finally questioned him as to why we had to stop at this location. He shared with me that this was his mother's house and he had to stop by every morning to get his younger brother out of the bed. Years ago at a family reunion, his brother, seven years old at the time, had been stung by a bee. Unfortunately, the result of that bee sting had left his younger brother a paraplegic. His father had been the initial Caregiver but had died years earlier from a terminal illness. However, before he passed, he had asked my friend to promise that he would take on the responsibility of helping his mother care for his younger brother. That was a promise he had kept for over 25 years and today he is still providing care for his younger brother.

Every morning, Monday through Friday, without fail, we would make this routine stop at this familiar house so that he could clean, dress and remove his brother from the bed. This made life just a little bit easier for his mother. He told me that he would perform that same task in reverse after he'd finished dinner at home with his wife and kids. Can you imagine performing this rigorous routine on a daily basis? Being a Caregiver myself, I had to ask the question, "How in the world can you go through this for twenty-five years and still maintain your sanity?" He admitted that it was not easy. There were times when he said that he wished for a normal life where he could relax and enjoy time with his family and friends after work or on the weekends. However, due to his brother's condition, it was not possible. He told me that there were times when he was alone in his bathtub when he would lay his head back, cover his face with his facecloth and cry. His duty as a Caregiver was a great burden, but he took this responsibility seriously and he made a promise that he could not go back on.

In 2009, his mother passed away, and now the responsibility of caring for his brother lies solely on him. Just recently I asked him how he was doing, and he answered by saying that "he didn't realize how good life was when his mother was alive." He at least had a few hours during the day to spend alone, but now his time belonged to his brother. His response was a reminder that we must always be careful to realize our blessings and to know that even in our darkest situations there is still another blessing to be found. My friend complained of not having enough time, but after the passing of his mother, he had no time. God is always blessing us in one way or another. Sometimes we see it clearly, but there are often times when we have to look through the darkness. My mother said it this way, "We complain of having no shoes until we meet the man with no feet." I think my mother was quite wise, don't you?

Chosen—we are more than conquerors

Just like my friend, we may come face to face with many challenges during the caregiving experience. We may even lose our focus as a result. However, those challenges come to make us strong. It is during those times that we must come to grips and recognize who we really are. It is in those moments that we must remember that we are more than conquerors. We are important. Everyone cannot do what we do because they do not have the strength or stamina required to fulfill the purpose. We are the chosen, and we have to acknowledge that Satan will try his best to deceive us and break us down. Do not fall into his trap of misconception. It is during these times that we need to step away, re-evaluate, and act on our belief that God will supply our every need. Let us not be fooled by the negative situations surrounding us (and believe me there will be many), but let us learn to choose our battles and turn things around for our own benefit (sanity). Many of us today are walking around, showing the world that we have been defeated. It's all right to sink into the realm of self-pity *occasionally,* but we can't fall in the pit and stay there. We have to get up and keep moving. Yes, we feel hurt; yes, we feel abandoned; and yes, we feel alone. God did not promise us a life full of happiness and joy. He allows trials and tribulations to test us, but He also allows us the use of His weaponry (His word) to win the battles. It is through our victories that we become stronger and wiser people. We are more than conquerors!

O Happy Day joy does come in the morning.

Scripture Reading:

Luke 10:19 *Behold, I give unto you power to tread on serpents and scorpions, and over all the power of the enemy and nothing shall by any means hurt you.*

Chapter Two

Why Me?

(The "Aha" Moment)

I am God's workmanship. For we are God's
workmanship, created in Christ Jesus to
do good works, which God prepared in
advance for us to do. Ephesians 2:10

As I mentioned earlier, some of us have asked the million dollar question, "Why me, how did I ever get here?" Well, I'm glad that you asked. After struggling to find the answer to this distressing question myself, I can venture to say that we got here because of the goodness in our hearts—that compassion that engulfs our spirits. Think about it for a moment. We are astonishing people who are naturally nurturing, instinctively motherly and put the needs of others before our own. Doesn't that describe us? And we wonder, "Why me?"

Grass is not always greener on the other side

As you put your life on hold to give care to others you may sometimes feel that you have deprived yourself of the happiness you deserve. It may appear that people are full of laughter and joy, and you sit in your small corner of the world providing care to an individual who could care less about your wants and wishes. Others seem free to enjoy life's pleasures without the shackles of caregiving to hold them back. They come and go as they please, have no demands on their lives, and do whatever they want, whenever they want. How dare they be happy while you are burdened with providing care? Why couldn't that be you? Well, let's stop here for a moment and think. Remember the old adage; the grass is not always greener on the other side? Keep in mind that people may put on happy faces, but many times they can be just as confused and conflicted with their lives. If we take a deeper look at our own situations and stop throwing little pity parties, we would realize something important. We are a chosen few. *"How is that possible?"* you may wonder! Well, let me explain a little something to you.

We have been prepared in advance for our role

Earlier I mentioned that caregiving is not something that we choose; however, it is something that we have been chosen to fulfill. Caregiving is a calling—a ministry so to speak—and it takes a special type of person to serve in that capacity. My personal belief is that the journey begins at childhood when we are groomed for the role. If you reflect on your own childhood, you may recognize a few clues of just how the caregiving plan was set in motion. You protected siblings, tried to please everyone, placed everyone's needs ahead of your own, and sacrificed your own joy so that others would be happy. Perhaps, if you were anything like me, you brought home a stray dog or two and even scattered day-old bread for the birds. Sound familiar? You were happy doing these things and expected nothing in return. So why would you expect any more today?

The "Aha" moment

There is an awesome joy that comes from serving others. Look at your situation. Imagine for a moment what God would have to say about your service. There is no doubt that after you hear what I am about to share with you, you will have an "*Aha!*" moment. My thought is that this passage, taken from the book of Ephesians, was written to give hope, especially to the Caregiver. Now get ready because it will blow you away. ***"For we are God's workmanship, created in Christ Jesus to do good works, which God prepared in advance for us to do."*** (2:10)

Aha! Didn't I tell you? Do these words not set you free? Do they not shine a brighter light on your situation? Think about it for a moment. Repeat it with me. "For we are God's workmanship, created in Christ Jesus to do good works, which God prepared in advance for us to do." Let those words marinate in your mind. Do they not lift the Spirit within you and make the burden of caregiving lighter? We have been *chosen* and *groomed* from the beginning for our role as Caregivers. This means that God has prepared us by implanting in us the "Spirit of Helps" and has placed us in a position to do His will—giving care to His people. Helps *(Note: The Spirit of Helps is just one of the many talents God gives.)* It is no coincidence that you are caring for someone today. God knew that this service would be required, so He prepared us and then sent us to do His work. It was all in His marvelous plan.

Your loving traits, your compassionate nature and your caring heart are the purposeful characteristics that God gave you and that make you special. They cannot be learned along life's journey; they are embedded in our human nature from the beginning as perfect gifts. Indeed, they are gifts of the Spirit. I'd like to believe these are special qualities that God sprinkled in as He formed us in our mothers' wombs, special gifts or "talents" that He equipped us with long before our arrival on earth. We have been created with special gifts of the Spirit which come to make us a *special* people.

O Happy Day! That's the answer to the painstaking question, "Why me?" God's workmanship—created in Christ Jesus to do good works, which God has prepared in advance.

Scripture Reading:

Psalms 139:13-14 *You made all the delicate, inner parts of my body and knit me together in my mother's womb. Thank you for making me so wonderfully complex! Your workmanship is marvelous—how well I know it.*

Chapter Three

Nothing Eases Pain like a Good Cry

(Tears Promote Healing)

*They that sow in tears shall
reap in joy. Psalms 126:5*

In the previous chapter, "Coming Face to Face with the Stranger," the episode that took place in the bathroom may have seemed a bit extreme to some of you. Rest assured, someone else has experienced the same or a similar situation and can truly relate to what I am trying to convey. It is a very real experience to lose you while caring for someone. However, realizing the truth and coming to grips with your role as a Caregiver is a step in the right direction to discovering new ways of making your situation better. Perhaps you are just starting out on your caregiving journey and have not yet found yourself in this particular situation. Be forewarned, challenges and situations such as these can and will occur. I am not saying that caregiving is a burden. Indeed, it can be a beautiful thing depending on how you perceive it; however, it can also be a heavy load to bear. I want you to put on the whole armor so that you can discern those challenges and be prepared to face them when they greet you unexpectedly. Those of us who have been on this journey for a while can agree that there are times that we find ourselves in circumstances that make us ask, "How did I ever get here?" Situations that are both frustrating and frequent—situations that make you want to cry.

God gave us tears as a mechanism of release

There is no denying the many stresses that come from giving constant and continuous care. Any time we extend ourselves to care for another human being, we will be presented with challenges that we must face. If there is no mechanism for release, these times can be explosive. The tasks that we perform on a daily basis may be one of many reasons God gave us the ability to cry. Crying releases sadness and stress, cleanses the spirit and gives us new insight—a look into what future steps we need to take in order to survive an ordeal. Why else would God provide such an amazing, emancipating instrument of protection if He didn't intend for us to use it? We deserve the release and we deserve the joy that the release can bring. So, when the burdens of life get so heavy that you can't cope, do yourself a favor and wash your worries away with a good cry. Let the heartbreak of pain, rejection, loneliness and despair escape through the tears you shed. Tears are our weapon of self defense to be used in the time of happiness and/or sadness. They are tools of deliverance to restore us back to health. Once the crying is over, there is a feeling of a renewed spirit, and things seem a wee bit better. It is priceless moments such as these where we indulge ourselves to release, renew and recover.

Tears will empty the vessel of impurities

Let me emphasize the importance of crying. It is the first step to victory and goes hand in hand with caregiving regardless of whether the tears are due to happiness, sadness or depression. Tears are not to be halted or confined on the inside; they are meant to be released. Have you ever felt the calm of flowing waters as you sat along a river's edge? Soothing, isn't it? Well, that is the same feeling you'll receive after you release the stored up negativity that fills you with despair. The liberation that comes from shedding tears is much like the serenity of flowing waters; it is a healing. So, I say, let the teardrops fall. As a sister Caregiver, I understand your pain; your feelings of loneliness, emptiness and despair; and the misunderstanding you face on a continual basis. As my grandma used to say, "ain't nothin' to ease the pain like a good cry."

The next step to victory comes through the rejuvenation process. Take a deep breath—*inhale*—breathe in the victory. Embrace it as it enters the body, relaxing your muscles, your mind and your spirit. *Exhale*—relinquish the impurities of negativity. Feel that negativity leave the body. Say goodbye to loneliness, envy, sadness and pain. Today you are becoming a new creature. Old things are passing away and behold, all things are becoming new. You are realigning the balance of hope and joy. Believe it, breathe it and find truth in it. You've emptied your vessel. You have purged out the sadness, and you are reviving the spirit. What a beautiful thing!

Weeping shall endure for a day, but joy, sweet joy, shall come in the morning.

Scripture Reading:

1 Peter 4:12-13 (KJV) *Beloved think it not strange concerning the fiery trial which is to try you, as though some strange thing happened unto you: But rejoice, inasmuch as ye are partakers of Christ's sufferings; that, when His glory shall be revealed, ye may be glad also with exceeding joy.*

Chapter Four

The Struggle
for Perfection
(Why Do I Feel So Guilty?)

*My guilt has overwhelmed me like a
burden too heavy to bear. Psalm 38:4*

The struggle to be perfect causes us an enormous amount of pain. It stems from guilt. But why do we feel so guilty? There is no other way to say this. We feel guilty because we are guilty. We are guilty of setting our standards too high. We are guilty of being too proud to ask for help. We are guilty of giving and giving until we want to give up. Finally, we are guilty of allowing our guilt to affect our ability to function. Striving for perfection is the perfect way to achieve failure. So why do we work so hard at trying to achieve it? Who are we trying to impress? What in the world are we trying to prove? And, what standard do we measure ourselves against? It is unfortunate that we back ourselves into a corner trying to achieve perfection without even realizing the truth: ***We are perfect***. Did you hear me? We are God's workmanship, and that in itself is perfect. Put that in the archive of your mind and refer to it whenever the need arises.

If you are finding it hard to believe that you are perfect, allow me to direct you to take a look at Hebrews 13:21 where Paul tells us this: "Now the God of peace, that brought again from the dead our Lord Jesus, that great shepherd of the sheep, through the blood of the everlasting covenant, ***make you perfect in every good work*** that is well pleasing in his sight . . . ." If that does not give you confirmation, I can't imagine what will. My goodness! Just think about it. You have practically "put your life on hold" to care for another human being, and yet you are filled with guilt! Do not allow your subconscious to overrule your common sense. Don't you realize that there is no better love than to lay down your life for a friend? What can be more perfect than sacrifice? The idea that you have to be the *perfect* Caregiver should not be adding to your frustrations.

As Caregivers, we must learn how to ask and receive help without feeling inadequate. Asking does not make us any more or less perfect, and striving to become perfect only adds stress and sickness to our everyday living. Learning to relax, to breathe and to keep our thoughts under control will assist us in retaining our sanity and physical health. We are each perfect in our own way and we have committed ourselves to providing care when no one else would take on the task. That's perfection in itself.

Feelings of guilt (and it is false guilt) are often Satan's way of attack. He sends those "fiery darts" to destroy our sense of worth as well as our self-esteem. However, if we study the Scriptures, we will know that God has already taken care of our guilt. Ephesians

1:4 says that "according as He hath chosen us in Him before the foundation of the world, that we should be holy and without blame before Him". We must continue to apply His word to our everyday living. In the Christian life there is no room for this false guilt, for in Christ Jesus we are blameless, consecrated, righteous, and justified. If we don't stand, or, "*back up on His word," as my dad would say*, we will most assuredly fall into the trap of feeling inadequate and inconsequential. False guilt is just one of the many feelings that come with the job of giving care. Do not let it taint your self-confidence because the effect of its negativity can be deadly.

Providing care for a loved one is a dutiful and demanding, 24/7 job. We are giving to the best of our abilities. Remember that no matter how hard you work today, there will always be something waiting for you tomorrow. So take your time, learn to relax and, most importantly, learn to feel good about yourself because you are important! Struggling with the thought of being imperfect will drive even the sanest person to the "nut house," and you'll be there all by yourself still feeling inadequate—still feeling as if you are a failure. Let them put you in a padded cell and see if anyone will be there to fulfill your job as a Caregiver. I don't believe that you will find one who can fill your shoes.

O Happy Day! God has made me perfect in every good work. Praise the Lord!

Scripture Reading:

James 1:2-4 *Dear brothers and sisters, whenever trouble comes your way, let it be an opportunity for joy. For when your faith is tested, your endurance has a chance to grow. So let it grow, for when your endurance is fully developed, you will be strong in character and ready for anything.*

Chapter Five

If You Don't Take Care of You, Who Will?

(You Deserve A Break Today—Really)

*And he said to them, 'Come away
by yourselves to a desolate place
and rest a while.' Mark 6:31*

The most important thing you can do as a Caregiver to ensure sustainable health is to schedule time for yourself. My pastor, a wise and influential man, once posed this question to me, "If you don't take care of you, who will?" That question stuck in my mind as if someone had chiseled it across my brain. Never had I thought of taking a break or asking for help. I just continued to let the frustrations grow and snowball until I wanted to explode.

You can't forget about yourself. You are the most important piece of this Caregiver's puzzle. Without you, the entire thing will fall apart. Frustration and anger build like plaque around your mental and physical health. They fester into illnesses and produce anxiety and depression. Have you ever had to struggle to take a breath? Have you ever had feelings of heaviness in your chest? There is a medical term for these symptoms. Both are examples of "anxiety attacks." They appear when you are overwhelmed with frustration and despair. They are indications that you are overextending yourself and that you need a break.

Our bodies were created to rest as well as work and to receive as well as give. However, as Caregivers, we oftentimes forget that our needs are just as important as those we serve and sacrifice our health for others. God does not want our lives to be consumed with weariness. He wants us to have a life of abundance, which means that He wants us to take time to be pampered, and ensure that we are strong, healthy and, yes, happy. I cannot emphasize enough the importance of scheduling time for you. It is virtually as important as breathing. We must allow time for some much needed R&R *(rest and relaxation)* because rendering care not only deprives us of our time, but it also strips us of our youth and vitality and makes us old and irritable. If every minute of the day is filled with caring for someone other than ourselves, how can we focus on our personal lives? You do acknowledge that you have a personal life, don't you?

It is so important that we begin to do what is necessary to ensure that our needs are also met. If that doesn't happen, we become incapable of helping others. Our spirits must be nurtured and nourished in order for us to remain healthy and productive individuals. Spending quality time alone helps to refuel and reconnect with the Spirit within us.

As we diligently go about the daily routine of changing linens, preparing meals, emptying bed pans, changing diapers, some of us also work eight-hour jobs, we become oblivious of the fact that our energies are being depleted. We tend to ignore the signs which result in "Caregiver burn-out,"—a symptom that comes from being overworked and overburdened. Instead of resting from our duties we continually push toward the next project until we find ourselves physically and mentally drained. We become like that little *Energizer®* bunny advertised on television that just keeps going and going and going . . . . Stop the madness! It's time to recognize that we cannot do it all. Sometimes we just need to say "No!"

Start today. Practice taking control of your life. Practice saying "no" while looking in the mirror. I have found that the easiest way to convey that message is to say it with a smile. Go ahead, try it, repeat after me, *"No, I'm sorry, but I am unable to do that at this time."* Another one, *"I'm sorry, but I can't find the time to do that just yet."* See how easy that was? Saying "no" with kindness in your voice will help people to accept rejection. My mother once told me that it is not what you say that will hurt a person but how you say it. It is the manner in which the message is delivered that will benefit the one doing the asking and also the one who is being asked. It is so significant that we learn to preface our negative responses with joy because joy will attract a positive reaction. It can also lighten the burden of guilt. Therefore, be amiable if you are unable to fulfill a request. Say "no" with a smile so that the person doing the asking doesn't walk away feeling hurt or rejected. *"I'm sorry, but I have too much on my plate right now. Maybe another time"* is a pleasant and simple response when you have to say "no."

There are also times when we have to ask for help. Why do we find that to be such a difficult thing to do? How often do we overload ourselves because we are afraid to ask for help? Perhaps *we* are afraid of being rejected. However, think about this: people will ask us to do almost anything, and we respond "yes" even when there is no more room on our plates. We will overwork ourselves to ensure that the request is met, even if it means denying ourselves in the process. Now ask yourself, "How crazy is that?"

The same principle applies to "asking" as it does to saying "no." It is something that we must learn over time. It takes practice. You can't imagine the number of family and friends who are willing to lend you a hand if only you would ask them. Asking is something we are not accustomed to doing, but it is something that we need to do if we are to avoid "Caregiver burn-out." Burn-out will keep us feeling frustrated and neglected. It breaks our spirits and makes us very bitter people. However, asking for help can eliminate negativity and add vitality to our lives. You would be surprised! Asking for help brings others into your world; along with that comes encouragement and free time to spend alone. Is there something you need help with today? This week? This month? Start with a small chore. Perhaps someone can pick something up from the store on the way home? Maybe you need someone to sit with a loved one for a couple of hours so that you can run some personal errands for yourself? There is someone willing and waiting to lend a helping hand. Asking for help is another step towards taking better care of you. Go ahead! Give it a try! *I dare you.*

Scripture Reading:

Proverbs 17:22 *A joyful heart is good medicine, but a broken spirit dries up the bones.*

Chapter Six

A Mother's Love
(Caring for an Angel)

But if any provide not for his own, and
especially for those of his own house,
he hath denied the faith, and is worse
than an infidel. 1 Timothy 5:8

Caring for my mother took the vast majority of my time; however, I must admit that it was one of the most rewarding and loving experiences of my life. Providing care for her was a simple and joyful task because she never complained, no matter what. She had a way of turning an ugly experience into a thing of beauty. I believe that her compassionate spirit was enhanced by her own experiences as a Caregiver to both her sister and mother. We live and we learn in this world and we have to be ready for whatever challenges we encounter.

I was a young girl when my mother cared for her sister. I remember when she turned her own bedroom into a sick room so that her sister could come to our house to live. Her sister had been diagnosed with stomach cancer and had become bedridden. However, instead of my mother placing her sister in a hospital or a nursing home, she made the decision to care for her in our home. My mother was a work-at-home mom; she made lamp shades for Stiffel and Company. Her daily routine consisted of rising at 5:45 a.m. to make breakfast for my father, send him off to work with a packed lunch, and then go to her workstation in the basement to begin her day of making lamp shades. Her schedule was 7:00 a.m.-3:00 p.m. (*Her workday was complete only after her soap operas were over: Guiding Light, As the World Turns, General Hospital, etc. We could not disturb my mother when her stories were on and the telephone had better not ring during this time because whoever the person on the other line was sure to get it.*) Once the clock struck 3:00 p.m., she would clean her area, turn off the lights and return upstairs to the kitchen where she would prepare the family dinner. Wow! What a mother (Note: I can't remember ever telling her how thankful I was for the way she cared for us. If you have that opportunity, please let your mother know how much she means to you). Once my aunt arrived, things didn't change much except mother had to check on her occasionally, change her, feed her and answer her bidding.

Watching my mother serve as a Caregiver to her sister was one of the most joyful and loving episodes of my life. She gave so much of herself in caring for her sister. She was often tired, but I never heard her complain, ever. I was truly blessed to have had an opportunity to witness this sharing of love between siblings because what came with it was a lesson in compassion. This experience taught me more about people than I would have ever imagined. It was truly a blessing for me to have been able to watch my mother in this capacity. Truly, it is one of the most significant lessons in my life.

In 1999 when mother was diagnosed with stomach cancer, those lessons that I had learned from her years earlier became valuable tools that carried over when I assumed my role as Caregiver. Mother suffered considerably from her cancer as it spread and soon metastasized to her bones. Six months after her diagnosis, mother was bedridden, and morphine became the perpetual tranquilizer for the pain she endured. Watching her transform from the beautiful woman she once was into an almost unrecognizable frame was heartbreaking. However, she never complained and only called if she wanted some company to sit and talk with her for a while. She maintained her loving spirit through it all.

I didn't have the opportunity to be at my mother's bedside when she made her transition. However, there were so many signals that prepared us for her demise. (I think that there are always signals.) One memory that I hold dear is, prior to her leaving us, she always asked for her shoes. She was obsessed with the idea of having her shoes on her feet. Each day when we would visit, her shoes would be her first request. My pastor commented that she wanted her shoes because in preparing for her transition, she needed her shoes for dancing; it is said that they dance for joy in Heaven. What a beautiful thought. Imagine the angels dancing, rejoicing and praising the Lord in celebration of another one of God's children making it home.

Another occurrence that I will remember is an incidence that one of mom's nurses shared with us. Nurse Armstrong said that as she was taking her vital signs, mom looked up at her and said, "I'm going home now". "You just rest Mrs. Glenn, you won't be going home today," she replied. Then, she left the room heading towards the nurses' station when she was approached by another nurse who told her to return to my mother's room to re-check her. When she entered mother's room the second time, she found her unresponsive. Mother had made her transition. She had done just what she had told Nurse Armstrong that she would do—she had gone home. She hadn't been talking about going to her earthly home; she was referring to the home in God's promise—the Father's house, with many mansions.

Scripture Reading:

John 14: 1-3 *Let not your heart be troubled: ye believe in God, believe also in me. In my Father's house are many mansions: if it were not so, I would have told you. I go to prepare a place for you. And if I go and prepare a place for you, I will come again, and receive you unto myself; that where I am, there ye may be also.*

Chapter Seven

Living with Dad
(A True Reality Show)

Cast me not off in the time of old age; forsake
me not when my strength faileth. Psalm 71:9

L et me tell you about a very special person in my
life, my daddy. It's not that I loved my mother any
less but I've always been a daddy's girl. After my mother
passed in July 2000, I had the honor of caring for my
dad. It wasn't an easy task, and God knows how many
times I got down on my knees in prayer during this
period in my life. I prayed as I left work, prayed on the
way home, prayed as I put the key in the door and prayed
as I entered the house. Dad would always sit in the back
room in his favorite chair, and as I put my things away
and greeted him from the kitchen, I would always hear
his voice welcoming me back home. "It's about time you
got here," or "where the h★★★ have you been" or, my
favorite, "you ought to know to bring your ★★★ home
sometime." My dad was a card. He would have driven
Jesus crazy if he had decided to one day pay him a visit.

Taking care of Dad could have been my ticket to
fame. I only had to add *lights, camera and action*. On many

occasions I thought strongly of placing video cameras throughout the house to capture those moments on film and produce a reality show called, *"Living with Dad."* I am certain that it would have been successful as it would have been full of comedy to make one laugh, drama to keep one in suspense and compassion to make one cry. Dad was a handful, full of the unexpected and, no matter what I did for him, it never seemed to meet his satisfaction. Have you ever tried your best only to find that your best was never good enough? Well, that was how it was with my dad. Don't get me wrong; I loved my daddy with all of my heart. They used to call me "daddy's girl." He was the best father in the world but was set in his ways and there was no changing his mind about anything. It was always his way or the highway.

Dad had always been the strength of our family. He provided the support, working two jobs, sometimes three, to ensure our needs were met and that we had a quality life. He was simply a man who loved his family and was unashamed to express his love for God and his church. He walked upright and told you the truth no matter how much it hurt. He was a man of many words, and some of them could cut like a knife. When he became ill shortly after the passing of my mother, I decided, once again, to take on the duty of Caregiver. (Why do we do such things?)

Taking care of dad could have been my chance of becoming a millionaire. I know in my heart that a show of this caliber, being the first and only reality show about caregiving would have blessed Caregivers throughout the nation as it would have been full of drama, comedy and suspense. My father was a character and very unpredictable. Walking through the door each day was a surprise. One day my daughter stayed home to watch him, and when she came downstairs to go into the kitchen, there he was standing in the nude frying up some bacon. Can you imagine the thought of a 92-year-old man standing at the stove butt naked? Oh, my God! My daughter screamed. "Why did this have to happen on my watch?" Needless to say, in the days to follow, she was very, very cautious when she entered any room.

My dad was a proud man. He denied that he was sick and insisted that he didn't need care. He became feeble and was unable to stand for long periods of time. However, his favorite place, before and after the nude scene, was at the sink in the kitchen, washing dishes. I swear to you that he would spend hours wiping the same countertops over and over, and I often wondered how the finish remained intact. But that was the place he wanted to be, and I allowed him to remain there for as long as he wanted because it would keep him occupied and gave me some quiet time. Most of his days were spent in that kitchen. Eventually, the time came when he could no longer stand or cook and I had to have someone come in during the day to ensure his safety.

I can remember coming home from work one day to find the venetian blinds were still closed, the house dark and Dad nowhere to be found. I went through every room of the house in search of him. Then, I went to the basement and found him lying on the concrete floor. He had fallen earlier that morning and couldn't get up. In his illness he had a habit of fixing things that weren't broken. That particular day, in his mind, the furnace needed fixing. My father had fallen and remained on that cold, concrete basement floor for over eight hours. That's when I realized I had some decisions to make. There will come a time in each of our lives when we must make decisions on the type of care and assistance that is needed for a loved one. Months prior to his fall, the doctors had diagnosed him with dementia but I was in denial.

The time finally came when Dad was bedridden. That was a very sad time for me, seeing my dad, once so strong and vibrant, now so frail and lethargic. My heart ached every time I looked at him lying in that fetal position on a hospital bed that had been moved into his room to accommodate his debilitating condition. He was unable to speak and his eyes, which had changed from brown to a glassy gray, would follow me across the room. He was always holding onto the rail of the bed as if he were clinging to life.

I had no problem when it came to the simple chores of washing Dad's face or cooking and feeding him; however, the question lingered in the back of my mind as to whether or not I would be capable of cleaning and changing diapers. I believe that is a question any child would ponder when caring for a parent. How would I be able to take care of his personal needs? As a daughter, I didn't believe I could clean the private areas of the body. That seemed far too personal and beyond my ability as a Caregiver. One day, when I was visiting my girlfriend who took care of her dad, I asked her how she got over that hurdle and she replied, "I have no idea how it happens, but God gives you the wisdom and the strength. You somehow just do what you have to do."

Well that turned out to be the holy truth. My god-sister worked as an aide in hospitals and rehab centers, caring for those who could not care for themselves. (You never know what you can learn from a person until the opportunity presents itself.) As a caregiver in the health facility, she was trained on how to care for people with debilitating diseases. The training that she gained through her experiences enabled her to teach me how to attend to my father's personal needs in a safe manner. With her help I was able to change and clean him, prevent anticipated bedsores, lift him without strain or injury and ensure his comfort and quality of life. Those words from my girlfriend echoed loudly as I found myself cleaning and changing my own father—I just did what had to be done, without hesitation.

Dad's illness got progressively worse and one night as I was lying on the sofa watching television, I clearly heard a voice say to me "go to your father's room and sit with him for a while." As I look back on that moment today I truly believe it was the voice of the Holy Spirit who beckoned me to visit Dad that night. As I entered his room, I found him in his preferred fetal position, holding onto the rail for dear life. His eyes opened slightly as I entered. "What are you up to?" I asked, and he slowly reached for my hand. Because he could no longer speak, he used his eyes to speak for him. I gave him my hand, and he slothfully lifted it to his lips and placed a weak but meaningful kiss upon it. "Oh, you love me today, do you?" I teased and he moved his head to signal "yes". I truly believe this was my daddy's way of letting me know that he did indeed appreciate everything that I had done for him. His illness seemed to have melted the shield of armor revealing the tender side of my dad that many had failed to see. Generally, he wasn't one to verbally express kind words, but in this vulnerable moment, he was telling me that he loved me. The gesture of a kiss upon my hand made all of the hell that I'd been through over the past few years worthwhile. This was his endearing manner of proof. I sat with him for over an hour and read from his favorite Bible and quietly sang a few of his favorite hymns. I knew that he listened attentively because whenever I forgot the words to the song, he would grunt as if to tell me that wasn't right. Even in his last hours, Dad had to have the last word, and I let him. We both enjoyed our time together that night. I could feel it in my spirit.

As the clock struck eleven, I told Dad that I was going to bed, kissed his forehead and told him that I'd see him in the morning. That was the last night we spent together. The next morning I rose from my bed as I had done so many times in the past and went into his room to prepare him for the day. There he lay in the same fetal position I had left him the night before. "Good morning, little darling," I sang, but he didn't respond. Daddy had slipped quietly away during the still of the night with the angels who had come to take him home.

God bless you Daddy! You probably won't believe this, but I've learned so much from our time spent together. Behind every dark cloud are moments to be cherished and lessons to be learned.

Scripture Reading:

Mark 7:10 (NKJV) For Moses said, 'Honor your father and your mother' and, 'He who curses father or mother, let him be put to death.'

Chapter Eight

In Our Darkest Hour God Will Send an Angel

(The Name is Insignificant)

A man of God came to me; he had the
appearance of an angel of God, terrible
indeed. I did not ask him where he came
from, nor did he tell me his name.
Judges 13:6

I remember when I was going through one of my most doleful stages as a Caregiver. My mind was filled with disparaging thoughts and it appeared that the Lord had forgotten me. Even more discouraging was the fact that people were still depending on me to save them from their own helplessness.

One cool Sunday morning I decided to escape for a few hours and treat myself to some quiet time. Stress had filled my world and sadness had taken residence in my heart. I needed the time to get away from reality to replenish my soul. I sat down at a table for two and was gazing out of the window attempting to evaluate my state of being, when I noticed a stranger approaching my table.

As one generally does, I dropped my eyes to my plate to avoid eye contact however; this stranger asked if he could take a seat. Although I hesitated at the thought of him invading my privacy, he quickly slid into the seat on the other side of the table and made himself comfortable.

He was a charming gentleman, nicely dressed on a Sunday morning as if headed to church. We just sat looking at one another for a few moments in silence; I was filled with query and he with trepidation. When he spoke, his voice was quiet and sincere. He expressed his concern that my being in deep thought had taken me to a dark place and that the Holy Spirit had directed him to come over to divert my sadness. Those few words caused tears to well in my eyes because it had been a long time since anyone had taken notice of me in that manner. Yet, this amazing stranger had come to comfort me in my time of weakness. How could he have known?

He reminded me that I was not alone in this world and that God, as our powerful Lord and Savior, would sustain me through everything, even when there seemed to be no hope. He then stretched out his hands and I placed mine cautiously in his while he offered up a prayer in my defense, right there in the middle of the restaurant. I felt the Holy Spirit move upon me to relieve me of my burden; I felt the warmth rise from the pit of my stomach, moving to ease the sadness that had engulfed my soul. When he finished his prayer, my spirit had been renewed. The burden had been lifted; I then realized that the stranger had been sent by God to help me through this dark hour of my life. I awkwardly thanked this stranger for his kindness and concern. He bid farewell and promised that "life would be good for me from then on". He then turned and headed toward the door. As I watched him leave, I thanked God again for His mercy and grace. When you're down and out without a clue of where your help will come from, know that God is there to intervene on your behalf. I truly believe that this stranger was a messenger sent from God.

God does hear our cries. He sends us angels to lift us from our darkness and into His light just when we need Him the most!

Scripture Reading:

Hebrews 13:2 *Be not forgetful to entertain strangers: for thereby some have entertained angels unawares.*

Chapter Nine

Give Love, Always
(Be an Unexpected Blessing to Others)

*And do not neglect doing good and
sharing; for with such sacrifices
God is pleased. Hebrews 13:16*

Love truly does make the world go around. It is a
gesture of caring and reaching out to others who,
at a certain period in life, are less fortunate than we are.
Whether we are demonstrating that love to an elderly
person, a child, a homeless individual or even a stranger,
it is something that, when given genuinely, will always
warm our hearts. Inevitably, we all will have our good
days and our bad days, and we don't know when they
will come; therefore, it is important that we remember
to continually reach out to others. My mother had a
saying that I will carry with me forever. "Treat people
with kindness because you never know who in this
lifetime will one day have to give you a piece of bread."
I have primarily based my life on those words, and they
often come back to haunt me when I hear of someone's
misfortune. I am certainly aware that there is no way

for me to help everyone, even if I died trying; however, there are times when the Holy Spirit moves me to perform small tasks for certain people and I trust that my obedience, in answering His call, will produce great results in their lives.

As I reflect on my life, it seems that over the years I have taken an interest in the elderly. They have become my *project,* so to speak. Perhaps it is because they tend to fall into the "forgotten" category. Or perhaps it is solely the joy that comes from giving. My heart aches to see sadness on the face of an elderly individual sitting alone in the park. My heart seems to ache when I visit a hospital and see the frailty of an elder lying helplessly unattended in a hospital bed covered with sheets that don't provide enough warmth. I recognize that many of our elders live alone and many have been placed into nursing facilities because taking care of them is too much of a burden for family members to bear. However, I never understood how people could be so insensitive as to put a loved one in a nursing home and, in some cases, forget to visit. Oh, my God! That says a lot about the character of a person. Don't get me wrong. There is nothing wrong with placing someone who requires constant, long-term care and attention in a nursing home. However, to drop someone there and forget that they even exist is inhumane.

After my parents were stricken with illness, it had never crossed my mind to tuck them away in some God-forbidden place to die. It wasn't something I had to think about as it was a *learned behavior,* a behavior that I chose to emulate as I watched my mother care for her own mother and sister. These were people who sacrificed their entire lives to love and care for our family, and now they were in the season to reap the harvest from the seeds they had sown. My choice to care for them was the seed they had planted in faith that their sacrifices would bring forth an abundant harvest of love and care. We all have a season. One day, sooner or later, we will have to reap what we sow. The book of Ecclesiastes 3:1-9 plainly tell us of the season. It reads like this:

> *To everything there is a season, and a time to every purpose under the heaven: A time to be born, and a time to die; a time to plant, and a time to pluck up that which is planted; A time to kill, and a time to heal; a time to break down, and a time to build up; A time to weep, and a time to laugh; a time to mourn, and a time to dance; A time to cast away stones, and a time to gather stones together; a time to embrace, and a time to refrain from embracing; A time to get, and a time to lose; a time to keep, and a time to cast away; A time to rend, and a time to sew; a time to keep silence, and a time to speak; A time to love, and a time to hate; a time of war, and a time of peace. What profit hath he that worketh in that wherein he laboureth?* And as we read further, verse 17 confirms that *God shall judge the righteous and the wicked: for there is a time for every purpose and for every work.*

Focusing on that scripture reassures me that sacrificing for the sake of others and serving as a Caregiver are both rewarding experiences. Reaching out not only helps another along his journey, but it will also build character and instills patience in the one who gives the care. There is a euphoric feeling of pride and purpose when you reach out to help someone. My mother would say that it is better that we "lend a hand up instead of give a hand out."

Chapter Ten

Forgiveness
(Learn to forgive those who seem to forget you)

And be ye kind one to another,
tenderhearted, forgiving one another,
even as God for Christ's sake hath
forgiven you. Ephesians 4:32

What could be more important than the Spirit of forgiveness? Why squander time and energy on unnecessary anger? Who are we actually angry with? The sister who doesn't seem to care? The brother who doesn't give of his time? The neighbor who spends time pampering herself? How silly is that? Don't you realize that harboring hatred and jealousy toward another individual is the best way to destroy yourself? Walking around with a loathsome attitude can eat away at the soul like a cancerous pustule waiting to erupt. People are so consumed with their own problems that they don't recognize that you are angry, why you are angry or whom you are angry with. In reality, we only hurt ourselves with such anger or animosity.

The one thing that most of us neglect to do as Caregivers is express our feelings to others. For some reason unbeknownst to me, we don't want people to know that we hurt and are in need of help. How can we expect to receive help when we don't reach out? Without verbally expressing ourselves we continue to be hurt and continue to ask the dreaded question, "Why me?" As I mentioned in previous chapters, asking for help is not a sign of weakness. For God's sake, let your request be known—ask!

People do not purposefully go out of their way to hurt us, neither is it their intention. Many do not give it a second thought as to what we go through on a daily basis because they simply have their own lives to manage. What are they to think? In most instances we make situations look so simple—we seldom complain, we're continually friendly and we wear that *pseudo* smile plastered across our faces indicating that "everything is all right." I am certain that many individuals in our circles of family and friends are willing to help, but we rarely give them the opportunity. Why? Because (*here comes those words again*) we feel guilty.

I learned the hard way. Anger consumed me. It took over my thinking ability and it changed me into someone I didn't recognize. However, when I came to my senses, when my caregiving days were over, I reflected back on those days. I came to realize that help was always there and I was to blame for my unwillingness to share in the responsibilities of caring for a loved one. Don't be like me. Learn from my mistakes and realize that when you don't ask for help, you are doing yourself a disfavor. When you refuse to accept the help that is offered, you limit, block or even steal a blessing that someone should be receiving. Imagine how much easier your life would be if you would just allow someone to enter into your world and lend a helping hand. Realize that there are others just like you who are looking for ways to share their blessings. We should not be so quick to keep them from doing so.

If you are harboring ill feelings toward someone today, I urge you to take a good look at the situation. Search yourself and then stop and analyze who's to blame. If it is a certain someone, forgive them. If it is you, forgive yourself and move forward. Forgiveness is such a crucial step in our quest to survive the caregiving experience. Jesus instructs us to forgive one another as our Father has forgiven us. Yes, it may be a hard mountain to climb, but once you reach the top you are able to see the situation clearly. The weight of the burden that has held us down for so long is lifted. What a bountiful blessing!

Chapter Eleven

There Is a Joy in Giving
(You will be rewarded richly)

He who is kind to the poor lends to the
LORD, and he will reward him for
what he has done. Proverbs 19:17

There is an enormous amount of joy that comes from caring for a loved one. Perhaps you can't conceive that just yet. The challenges that we face on a daily basis may be the culprits that keep us from realizing those joys. In order to realize those joys, we have to first let go of the negative energies that keep us locked in despair. Jealousy, envy and other worthless feelings of despondency that may dominate our thoughts only keep us shackled to hopelessness. The results that come from harboring such hostilities drain us of our happiness and keep us in a holding pattern of misery. Thoughts such as these will keep us drowning in a cesspool of self-pity and destruction. We must not allow Satan to exercise his power to bamboozle us into becoming our own worst enemies. The release of those destructive powers that enslave us can help clear the way to a substantial life. Stop holding onto negative thoughts; the devil is a liar!

We are often our own worst enemy, holding on to ugliness that keeps us trapped and in bondage. We have to remove the blinders in order to see God working in us. We cannot see the entire picture while holding on to hostile emotions that waste our time and keep us from reaching our full potential. God wants you to move forward and reach your true destiny. Eliminating negative thoughts from our minds will free us from anxieties and remorse and allow us to focus on the many rewards that God is bestowing upon us.

Being that support person who provides care for aging parents, grandparents, siblings, spouses or other loved ones, should bring us joy. Remember that we are the chosen vessels, sent by God to encourage and support others in their times of weakness. For many, we are the life line to survival, doing for them what they cannot do for themselves. Although the role we play as Caregiver may be difficult, God continues to grant us the courage and strength needed to *press toward the mark for the prize of the high calling of God in Christ Jesus (Philippians 3:14 KJV)*. We have to keep moving, finding strength in knowing that we have been sent by God to perform duties and remain proud of the fact that we have been chosen. We must stay strong, equipped with a helping hand, a loving heart, and a kind word to provide comfort and compassion in times of unforeseen circumstances. To know that we are Heaven-sent should provide us with that unspeakable joy of which choirs sing.

We are such a blessed people. Think on this: while we share our love with others in the form of compassion, God is sharing his love with us. He gives us everything we need to survive our journey. However, unless we release those barriers that hinder us from feeling God's presence, we will never realize His joys. Remember that God has made us a special people; we perform our roles for Him. He will never leave us nor forsake us. Believe on that. Breathe it, inhale it and anchor those words deep within your heart. It is His holy truth.

God has sanctioned us to care for His people. Just as He fed the hungry, cared for the sick and saved those that were lost, He has empowered us to do the same. Isn't that a wonderful blessing to enjoy and share with others? Indeed it is! What a thought to ponder! Yes! There is an enormous amount of joy that comes from serving and caring for God's people. And you do it with great generosity. What a blessing to behold and what rewards await us when we reach the Holy Jerusalem.

Chapter Twelve

Relax—Make Yourself a Priority
(Spend time enjoying life)

*And which of you by being anxious can add a
single hour to his span of life? Matthew 6:25*

Jesus said that the second most important commandment
in the Old Testament was to love our neighbors as we
love ourselves. Loving yourself is not a selfish act unless
you choose to love yourself more than others. But, how
can we love ourselves if we continually neglect our own
needs?

We live in a fast-paced society where every day
we are rushing to complete one task after another. We
seldom take time to talk with one another or listen to
what others are saying. Oh, we hear them, but do we
actually listen? We dash off to work, endure traffic jams,
and once we enter the workplace, we rush the clock so
that we can return home again to the same monotonous
routines. We are in a constant struggle to juggle. We have
become robotic.

Have you ever researched the word robotic? It describes something as being mechanical, programmed, humorless, uncaring, insensitive and preset to perform. It seems unbelievable, but it is so true. We have become robotic creatures. Some of us go through life performing the same routines every day without a second thought as to how robotic our lives have become. We never realize that we are losing out on so much more that life has to offer. Many of us are living in a robotic state. We are in a constant hurry but what are we actually accomplishing? We are just carrying on mechanically.

We need to slow down. What's the rush? Whatever doesn't get completed today will still be there beseeching our attention tomorrow. As Caregivers, it is important that we begin to rehabilitate ourselves so that we are not animated individuals performing the same routines on a daily basis. We have to learn to break the monotony of rushing through life. Choosing to slow down will allow us to focus on those little things that get placed on the back burner, those things that give us joy and make life worth living.

If we slow down a bit, we will have more opportunities to enjoy all that life has to offer. We miss so much as we speed through the day. As we begin to slow down, it is important that we also turn the focus on ourselves. As Caregivers, we deserve some "me" time, so that we are able to move from a mundane way of living to one that is bursting with balance and harmony. So how do we do that, you ask? Well, it doesn't happen overnight. It is something that we must put into practice. Some of us have lived in subtlety for so long that we don't see it any other way. However, the addition of a little selfishness toward our personal needs can make the difference between just existing and living life to the fullest. For starters, we have to stop feeling that because we are Caregivers we have no life outside of providing for others. Where in the world does that idea come from? Realizing that "Caregiver" is a title and not a way of life is the key to recognizing that we have a right to an abundant life just like others. Our lives did not end once we took on the role, so why are we stuck in the rut of believing that it has?

Slow down, evaluate and determine how you can make life better for yourself. Start with small gestures. If you have a spouse, plan a candlelit dinner. It doesn't have to be an elaborate feast; a pot of chili, a pan of cornbread and a tossed salad will suffice. Enjoy an evening walk while holding hands to regenerate old feelings that got lost somewhere between "I have to take care of . . . and, I don't have time to . . . ." Are there children that you may have neglected? Maybe it's time to spend some time enjoying an ice cream sundae or baking some chocolate chip cookies. Even if you live alone, you can enjoy an opportunity to pamper yourself. Draw a scented, bubble bath, light some candles, or just sit back with a book or magazine that you've been longing to read. Whatever your situation, find a way to change things for your benefit so that you can enjoy some *"quality"* time with yourself. Little by little you will find that slowing down and spending time with yourself brings so much peace of mind.

Quiet! Listen! I believe I can hear the birds singing . . .

Chapter Thirteen

You're entitled to A Stress Free Life

(Yes, You Have Rights!)

> *Cast your burden upon the LORD, and He will sustain you; He will never allow the righteous to be shaken. Psalm 55:22*

Y ou have the right to a happy and healthy life just as anyone else does. A list, granting permission to do things that will to help to alleviate stress, is provided here. Using this list will help you to re-focus and assist you in discarding some of that guilt that encompasses your daily routine. It will help you to remember that your schedule must include time for YOU. What good is a day when you don't spend any time focused on YOU? Hopefully the statements below will place an emphasis on regaining your self-esteem and allow you to realize that you are indeed an important part of the caregiving equation. Remember the question, "If you don't care for yourself, who will? You were made to have life and live it abundantly. That includes the right to be healthy, happy and prosperous even while being a Caregiver. The following is a pledge to remind you of your importance. Review it daily to keep you focused.

I Promise to:

- Schedule time for myself. There is absolutely nothing wrong with going to the spa, having a pedicure, manicure or even a one hour massage. I deserve it, and I promise myself this pampering experience.
- Believe in myself. I know that I am worthy, and I will treat myself with respect and honor.
- Get angry. Anger is natural and if not released will become toxic and destroy me and everything around me. Stress causes physical and mental disparities, and I will not allow negative feelings to creep into my mind and remain. I will use tears whenever necessary as a form of release, and I will not feel guilty about doing so.
- Take care of me. I will not put others before my own health, sanity or mental stability, and I will remember the question, "If you do not take care of YOU who will?"
- Believe that I am PERFECT. We are perfect creatures created by God, and God does not make mistakes.
- Ask for help. Asking for help is not a sign of weakness. It is a signal that I want to share this caregiving experience with others around me so that they can feel the joy that comes from giving.

- Feel guilty about things I do or don't do. I understand that guilt is one way that Satan attempts to make me feel defeated and inferior.
- Always forgive others. Although it is natural to feel abandoned by family members and friends, I vow not to let negative feelings turn me into someone I don't desire to be because I realize that no one can understand the role that I play just like no one can fill my shoes. I realize that forgiveness cleanses the spirit and opens the door to absolute blessings.
- Stay focused and encourage myself to accomplish my role as Caregiver. It takes courage to step into this world, and I deserve the right to reward myself as often as necessary.
- Thank God for His many blessings, seen and unseen, while I am on this Caregivers' journey.
- Count it a joy to care for a loved one and a privilege that I have been selected to fulfill this role. "Many have been called, but few are chosen".
- Be proud that God has prepared and ordained me to take on this role and learn from this experience so that I am able to share with others.
- I will encourage myself even though the mission may seem impossible.

Chapter Fourteen

When Your Faith Is Tested
(Be Grateful That You Are One of the Chosen Few)

*Dear brothers and sisters, whenever trouble
come your way, let it be an opportunity
for joy. For when your faith is tested, your
endurance has a chance to grow. So let
it grow, for when your endurance is fully
developed, you will be strong in character
and ready for anything. James 1:2-4*

Dear Brother and Sister Caregivers:

Life presents itself in a variety of ways—anger,
happiness, frustration, envy, hatred, wonderment,
kindness and joy. But there is one thing in life that stands
tall above them all, and that is love. We live in an age of
uncertainty, but when the day is over, when the lights
have dimmed, when closed eyes are sleeping and we reflect
on the day, we realize that no matter how frustrating our
trials, no matter the number of disappointments we've
faced or how much our hearts may have ached today, love
conquers all things. As we lie down tonight to reflect on

our days we will think about how we brought happiness to another human being through our gift of giving.

As Caregivers, we acknowledge that every day will find someone waiting to be cared for and every day someone will answer the call to render that care. There are some who require more care than others, some who can dress themselves and some who are waiting to be dressed. Some will rise to greet the day, but there will also be someone waiting for that special person to click on the light, greet them with a smile and attend to their personal needs. Whether or not they smile back is unimportant because we will know in our hearts that they are grateful for the presence of a Caregiver. Regardless of whether they speak kind words of gratitude or hurtful words of disfavor, we will know in our heart of hearts that we are appreciated because we have chosen to give.

As Caregivers, we may get weary, we may feel alienated and, often times, we may be saddened by our situations. However, in our hearts we stand firm in believing that *behind every dark cloud* is a silver lining, and through it all we will not give up because God has prepared us for this journey. He has given us everything we need to fulfill the task. It is because of His will and not ours that we carry out His plan. Is there anything more important in this life than to carry out God's purpose? I think not.

I don't doubt that weariness will fall upon you; therefore, I persuade you that when and if it does, you will deliberate on the words found in this little book and be encouraged. When the need for an emotional release arises write it down. Writing helps us to discover things about ourselves that we fail to otherwise realize. It is a wonderful form of therapy.

I truly pray that this book has been a lamp unto your feet to help you discover more than ever the importance of your presence in the lives of those you serve. Caregiving is not an easy assignment and not many can fulfill the call. You have been appointed by the High and Mighty King of Kings, and because of this you will be blessed, and you will be victorious. I love you for who you are and how you will overcome. Be joyous!

God bless you and keep you always.

Your sister in caregiving,

Chapter Fifteen

"Scriptures to Savor"

If you then, evil as you are, know how to give good and advantageous gifts to your children, how much more will your Father Who is in heaven [perfect as He is] give good and advantageous things to those who keep on asking Him! *Matthew 7: 11*

Cure the sick, raise the dead, cleanse the lepers, and drive out demons. Freely (without pay) you have received, freely (without charge) give. *Matthew 10: 8*

In everything I have pointed out to you [by example] that, by working diligently in this manner, we ought to assist the weak, being mindful of the words of the Lord Jesus, how He Himself said, It is more blessed (makes one happier and more to be envied) to give than to receive. *Acts 20: 35*

Give, and [gifts] will be given to you; good measure, pressed down, shaken together, and running over, will they pour into [the pouch formed by] the bosom [of your robe and used as a bag]. For with the measure you deal out [with the measure you use when you confer benefits on others], it will be measured back to you. *Luke 6: 38*

He who sows sparingly and grudgingly will also reap sparingly and grudgingly, and he who sows generously [that blessings may come to someone] will also reap generously and with blessings. *2 Corinthians 9: 6*

For God is not unjust so as to forget your work and the love which you have shown toward His name, in having ministered and in still ministering to the saints. *Hebrews 6:10*

But he said to me, "My grace is sufficient for you, for my power is made perfect in weakness." Therefore I will boast all the more gladly about my weaknesses, so that Christ's power may rest on me. That is why, for Christ's sake, I delight in weaknesses, in insults, in hardships, in persecutions, in difficulties. For when I am weak, then I am strong. *2 Corinthians 12:9-10 (NIV)*

Not that I speak in respect of want: for I have learned, in whatsoever state I am, therewith to be content. I know both how to be abased, and I know how to abound: every where and in all things I am instructed both to be full and to be hungry, both to abound and to suffer need. I can do all things through Christ which strengtheneth me. *Philippians 4:11-13*

Bear one another's burdens, and thus fulfill the law of Christ. *Galatians 6:2*

Love is patient; love is kind. Love is not jealous; is not proud; is not conceited; does not act foolishly; is not selfish; is not easily provoked to anger; keeps no record of wrongs; takes no pleasure in unrighteousness, but rejoices in the truth; love bears all things, believes all things, hopes all things, and endures all things. *1 Corinthians 13:4-7*

A Chosen Vessel

Bernita Ann Glenn

It is not because of me that I carry this
smile upon my face;
Have enough joy to fill the saddest place.
A tongue that sings the sweetest song;
And a peace that abides should all go wrong.

I have gladness in the place of sorrow;
Good hopes and dreams for a better tomorrow.
The Master's word deeply rooted in my heart;
To shield me from Satan's fiery darts.

It is not on my own that I smile through the tears;
Or focus on strengths and rarely the fears.
That I walk with the Lord whose love is forever;
And feel secure in the thought that He'll leave me never.

It is not because of me that I carry these things;
It is because I am a chosen vessel.

About the Author

B ernita A. Glenn is a Caregiver whose experience is based on years of caring for both her mother and father. Knowing, first hand, the difficulties associated with caring for a loved one, she was motivated to share her story in the hopes of making the journey an easier one for others. She has inspired many through the Caregivers Ministry at her church and is searching for additional ways to encourage and uplift those who have been challenged by the efforts of rendering care. She is available as a workshop presenter to instruct churches and community organizations on how to build a Caregivers Ministry.